AN EAGLE'S FLIGHT

MY JOURNEY FROM FEAR TO FREEDOM

DEBORAH McCAFFERTY

MW01145062

AN EAGLE'S FLIGHT – MY JOURNEY FROM FEAR TO FREEDOM
BY DEBORAH MCCAFFERTY

Copyright © 2017 Deborah McCafferty. All rights reserved. Except for brief quotations for review purposes, no part of this book may be reproduced in any form without prior written permission from the author.

Published by:

 LIFEWISE BOOKS

PO BOX 1072
Pinehurst, TX 77362
LifeWiseBooks.com

Interior Layout and Design | Yvonne Parks | PearCreative.ca

To contact the author:
DeborahMcCafferty.com

ISBN (Print): 978-1-947279-01-8
ISBN (Kindle): 978-1-947279-02-5

Printed and bound in Canada

DEDICATION

To my husband Rod,
and our children, Bailey, Kelsie & Connor.

Forever xoxo.

TABLE OF CONTENTS

INTRODUCTION

Fear was never meant to be a companion.

After spending three decades in an ongoing relationship with fear, leaving that relationship has enabled me to look back, examine my life, and see fear for what it really is. Fear is toxic, eager to knock on life's door and show up for a short visit, or move right in for an extended stay. I experienced both for far too long, and supplied fear with copious amounts of my time, energy, feelings and focus.

I don't believe any of us would choose to empower this type of relationship if we understood the scope of what was being empowered. None of us would deliberately open our front door to a thief and say, "Come on in, take whatever you want, and I'll sit over there in the corner of my couch while you do." Fear works overtime to disable the likelihood of living the abundant life with a prosperous soul.

On the other hand, pursuing and maintaining a relationship with freedom is courageous, satisfying, life-giving, and well worth it.

Freedom has encouraged me to step out, create, be me, and live an abundant life with a prosperous soul. Freedom extends a well-crafted, beautiful invitation to live life beyond what we can think or imagine, and I am forever grateful I have received and can share the invitation.

I'm honored you would take time to read the words I've written in the pages that follow as I share my journey with fear, from my early years to where I am today. This journey has led me from fear to freedom, from unbelief to belief, and saying yes to the most important relationship I will ever know: a relationship with God, whose love for you and me is unfailing.

I had no idea how to begin writing chapter one and wondered more than once if I would have enough words to fill a page. I have predominantly been a stay-at-home mom for seventeen years, and the extent of my writing has been journaling dreams or attempts to record thoughts in different seasons. Shortly after committing to the writing process with Charity Bradshaw, curiosity had me search for any video of her grandmother Frances Hunter, whom she had mentioned. I chose one to watch and a couple of minutes into the online video, Frances said, "A miracle is worth a million words." I had received miracles, and although I may not have a million words to write, I have enough to confidently share I am now living free from severe anxiety, panic, and depression. No longer struggling with my mental health. It's possible!

Today, I haven't run to my bedroom overcome with panic as I had multiple times in the past. Instead, I casually sit on our bed to write a few final thoughts on this part of my journey, savoring the stillness of the day and the view out our window. The sky is slightly overcast with a hint of blue, and a slight breeze moves the branches of a nearby tree. I can hear the occasional chirping of a bird and a plane flies overhead in the sky as I give thanks and enjoy it all with a quiet mind.

CHAPTER ONE
IT'S ABOUT LOVE

As far back as I can remember, babies have brought me delight.

The opportunity to cradle a little one in my arms has always been time well spent. The reward that accompanies connecting tenderly with new life is a fresh encounter with a sacred space—a God-given space bathed in love and peace, saturated by His very breath. In this atmosphere, awe and wonder are the ingredients to beholding and valuing how precious life is.

This same awe can be experienced when examining a clear, starry night sky, the same sky a childless Abraham stood before in Genesis 15:5 as God spoke this promise: "Look up at the sky and count the stars—if indeed you can count them." Then He said to him,

"So shall your offspring be." Abraham's faith was stirred by creation, even when not understood or yet seen. Every life is as magnificent as the stars in the sky. Every life is stamped with heaven's approval, promise, and love long before we are held in someone's arms.

Recognizing Love

As a young girl, it would not have been unusual to find me leaning over a stranger's stroller, enamored by the days-old infant from next door or struggling to carry a toddler half my size around our neighborhood. Today, you can still find me leaning over the stroller of an unfamiliar newborn, striking up a conversation with the expectant mom in the cereal aisle, or sneaking a peak in the grocery cart that's been taken over by a car seat.

My husband and I had our shopping carts overtaken during our early years of marriage by the arrival of three incredible children. With awe and wonder, we welcomed two very beautiful daughters and a handsome son. I have sweet memories of holding each one of them close to my heart for extended cuddle times during their first years, intentionally filling their new lives with loads of affection. Every minute spent studying their unique features and wildly cheering them on in their attempts to conquer their firsts was immensely satisfying. Watching my children grow has never become old or uninteresting, but rather has taught me valuable lessons: identity, patience, perspective, the value of time, and how God feels about me.

Years would pass before realizing the love I had felt while holding my children close or wrapping my arms around the child of another was a measure of the immeasurable love God had for me. Even before I knew Him, I was acquainted with His love, and when love seemed to have alluded me during difficult seasons, God who is Love had been with me the entire time.[1]

As I had gazed upon and diligently watched my children grow, He had been gazing upon and watching me, patiently waiting for a love connection between us. He was waiting for that moment of connection when I would realize my ability to sense, feel, receive, be overwhelmed by and give away love had everything to do with God loving first.[2]

On a random day in 2011, flipping through a photo album comprised mostly of pictures from my childhood, I stopped suddenly at a picture of myself around eight months old. I had looked at this picture before, but this time I noticed something I had never seen. The orange shag carpet and flowered, oversized chair decorated in shades of browns and golds, were the backdrop to something greater to be seen, a beautiful smile. As I deliberately looked closer, it struck me that God's intentions towards me have always been and always will be good. The joy captured on that day, during my first year of life, was a joy available from the very beginning, stretching into my todays.

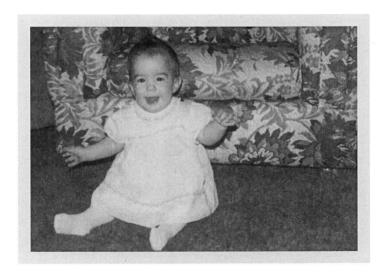

Walking through emotional pain, battling severe anxiety, panic, depression, and fighting for my mental health wasn't a cruel joke from a God who wanted to mislead me in this life. His love was real, had been there before my beginning, and was constant whether I had believed in Him or not. Before knitting me together in my mother's womb, I had been, just as you are and will always be, His priority and delight:

> "You saw who you created me to be before I became me!
> Before I'd ever seen the light of day,
> The number of days you planned for me
> Were already recorded in your book.
> Every single moment you are thinking of me!
> How precious and wonderful to consider
> That you cherish me constantly in your every thought!
> O God, your desires toward me are more
> Than the grains of sand on every shore!
> When I awake each morning, you're still thinking of me."[3]

Early Years

It wasn't uncommon in my elementary school years to awaken my parents in the night with a stomachache. After visits to the doctor, my mom would conclude the stomachaches were a result of worry. Early on I could have been described as overly sensitive, shy, serious, and a perfectionist. In addition to those qualities, I could have also been described as creative, intuitive, compassionate, and on occasion, funny. Unfortunately, I grew to focus more on what I believed were the less desirable, misunderstood qualities about myself. Eventually this would lead to identifying with labels such as *sensitive* that made me feel small.

Being bullied in elementary school inflated my insecurity and shrouded me with a sense of never quite fitting in and feeling like an outsider, uncertain of where I belonged. The pursuit of perfection throughout those early years put unnecessary pressure on myself, resulting in tremendous difficulty with writing tests, completing certain assignments, and contributing ideas. The more difficult these tasks became, the more I believed I wasn't smart but stupid. This lie became difficult to overcome as future challenges built the case in my mind that I most definitely was not bright. I was continually troubled that I couldn't remember facts with ease, but I could remember a moment by feeling.

At the tender age of twelve, I privately entertained thoughts that maybe my life wasn't worth living. As I entered my teen years, daydreaming about life was easier than participating in it. Daydreams about the kind of girl I wished I were minimized who I already was. The message that I was not good enough swirled within my developing mind. Perfectionism became procrastination, and I learned early on I couldn't fail at what I didn't try.

Every so often, a friend would comment on my worrying, but I would shrug it off, not having insight into the breadth of the problem. If only I had known, worry was the problem, not me. Escaping to my bedroom became a regular pastime, spending hours listening to music so that I could disappear inside the lyrics and beat of a song. Little did I know, God would later use music to break into my heart as a young adult.

My inner world was developing rapidly, mostly influenced by my inside voice and another voice that I would discern as an adult had never been mine. The enemy had been speaking, too. Led by strong emotions and deep thinking, the thoughts I meditated on were not encouraging, nor did they promote the development of my identity. Under the surface, I was a young lady craving love, acceptance and affirmation.

I Am God's Plan

Raised in a non-Christian home where God was not mentioned, I first knew Jesus as the baby who lay in the manger at Christmas. Our Christmas traditions included believing in Santa Claus, one my husband and I continued with our own children. On Christmas Eve, I have memories of my brother and I standing on our beds, peeking out the window, determined to catch a glimpse of Santa riding his sleigh through the sky. We were convinced we could hear bells jingling in the distance, the excitement mounting while we watched Frosty the Snowman on the television. Carefully plated cookies, milk and carrots were placed on the hearth for Santa and his reindeer, and bedtime would really mean tossing and turning for the rest of the night, excitedly awaiting Santa's arrival.

In my opinion, my parents' Christmas tradition wasn't wrong. I wasn't devastated when I finally realized that a large man, dressed in a red suit bearing gifts wouldn't be coming down our chimney. However, it does confirm that we are wired to believe that the supernatural exists, and the supernatural is God. We did not realize He was available for a brother and a sister looking to the sky, watching for what they couldn't see.

Around the age of nine, I remember feeling an unusual disappointment at the end of Christmas Day. Not because we hadn't received good gifts, special treats, or gathered around the dining room table for turkey dinner. Those traditions had all happened, and the disappointment wasn't selfish. It was a disappointment on the inside, a sense of something missing that would continue to repeat itself at the passing of each Christmas.

It wasn't a void to be filled by my parents, future husband, children, or friends. Rather, it was a void that needed to be filled by God Himself, who would intervene along the way because I was His. Intervention looked like me at age ten sitting early in the morning as close to our television as I could possibly get. My family slept while I was drawn to a show that kept my attention with its songs, characters, and spirit. The show was called *Circle Square*, a Canadian Christian television program broadcast for kids by Crossroads Christian Communications. I don't know how many times I would sit in front of our television to watch this show, but today I still remember the address that was sung at the end of each program.

Ultimately, you and I are God's plan, and I have learned He doesn't give up on, forget about, or tease us with His plans. He who created the dark-eyed, dark-haired baby girl had a plan. Even as that baby grew into an elementary school girl riddled with worry, an anxious teenager, and a fearful young woman, faithfulness had a plan.

At the right time, this plan included introducing me to His son. He wanted me to know the baby I had sung about in Christmas songs, who I had seen lay in the manger year after year. God would show me the same faith required to believe that reindeer flew in the sky was the same faith required to believe in His Son.

"For I know the plans I have for you," declares the Lord,
"plans to prosper you and not to harm you, plans to give you
a hope and a future."[4]

A Child's Mind—Healthy & Strong

A great future is comprised of great thinking.

I believe one of the greatest gifts we can offer our children is to closely walk with God. We need to foster homes and church communities filled with men and women who think and speak in extraordinary ways, with words that allow us to inspire, influence and change the world around us. Healthy thinking includes being mindful about the books we choose to read, the shows we watch, who we listen to, how we spend our time, who we spend it with and these days, what we Google.

As a child, I didn't know I could take my thoughts captive. I didn't realize I was meditating excessively on thoughts that were harming me and my intended future. I received wounds from people that impacted my thoughts but I also hurt my soul unintentionally every time I believed a negative thought about myself. I had experienced bullying from others, but have you ever realized, every time you put yourself down you are bullying yourself?

Our thinking and feeling can really determine our days. For example, between the ages of eight and twelve, I frequently would awaken in the night afraid and not tell my parents. Sometimes I had dreams that would scare me, and on occasion I would see spirits, or what I may have called ghosts, in my room lined up alongside my bed. My solution included lying on my side and pulling the sheet up over my ear to feel safe. The longer I focused on being scared, the more scared I would become. My imagination would take me on a journey that I never needed to go on, and if I had watched a horror movie, which happened during those years, scary thoughts would be heightened. How different it might have been, if I had learned early on to say "no" to that journey and sleep with peace.

In December of 2016, I witnessed a "no" from a three-year-old girl. We were visiting with friends in our home on a cold Saturday morning, taking time out to sip cider, enjoying one another's company and the season. One of the families in our living room included four incredible girls. While the older girls initially engaged in crafts and coloring, their three-year-old requested to play in our basement. She had visited our basement before, which is a fully developed, pleasant space. There were no visible dangers, and her fear wasn't warranted, but on this occasion, as I opened the door and took her hand, as quick as her little foot shot out to take a step, she spoke, "I'm scared." The words had left her mouth, but without missing a beat, she looked up at me, into my eyes and said, "No, I'm not scared. God is with me all the time."

She had been taught truth and how to think.

"Have I not commanded you? Be strong and courageous. Do not be frightened, and do not be dismayed, for the Lord your God is with you wherever you go."[5]

I'll be honest—her words caught me off guard, and time suspended long enough to comprehend what I had heard. I honor my friends, as they parent their children with truth—truths they will one day pass on to their children's children.

I had held her hand that day, but so had God as He reminded her of who He is.

"For I am the Lord your God who takes hold of your right hand and says to you, do not fear; I will help you."[6]

She played in the basement that day, and fear didn't cause her to miss out. When the visit came to an end, guess who didn't want to leave? If it's possible at three, it's possible at any age for our thinking to be filled with truth and respond courageously to fear.

"Finally, brothers and sisters, whatever is true, whatever is noble, whatever is right, whatever is pure, whatever is lovely, whatever is admirable—if anything is excellent or praiseworthy—think about such things."[7]

Our future depends on it.

"You'll Be OK"

Multiple times, the Bible reminds us that God is with us, helps us, and will never leave us, and just as a very bright three-year-old reminded me, I had also found out as a teenage girl just how much God is with me.

On a summer's evening, in July of 1988, age fifteen, I was hanging out with friends. We were trying to decide where we wanted to go that night. My dad during this time was a member of the Royal Canadian Mounted Police, and we only had a couple of weeks left in our current small town posting before our family was to move.

Leading up to this night, I had gone out on a couple occasions without my parent's permission. On this particular night, my friend and I had lied about where we were spending the night to extend our curfew. We thought we were setting up a night of freedom, but fear had another plan. My friend was old enough to drive and had her own vehicle, so three of us girls set out to enjoy the evening. Mostly cruising, sometime after midnight we stopped in the parking lot of a community centre and picked up three male friends. The big plan after picking up the boys was to drive ten minutes to the twenty-four-hour convenience store across town to get something to eat.

I sat on the lap of one of our male friends in the middle of the back seat. We sped off in the direction of the store on a dark country road as pouring rain blanketed the front windshield and music blasted in our ears. Minutes into the drive, the boy whose lap I sat on requested we switch places. He was now sitting on my lap and I found myself sitting in the middle tucked between three teenage boys.

Not long after switching places, I attempted to peer around the shoulder of the boy sitting on my lap. I was trying to make eye contact with the front window of the car, sensing that something was wrong. The driver was losing control of the vehicle. I opened my mouth to scream but was gently silenced by a voice that spoke clearly into my right ear: "You'll be OK." I had never heard this voice before, and as quickly as the words came, I closed my eyes, bowed my head, and felt a wave of peace wash over me that put me into what I can best describe as a deep sleep.

I don't remember the car crashing through the fence posts or flipping several times through the farmer's field. I came to, with what would have been the car's final thud as it took its place upside-down on the mud-soaked ground. Fear rushed through my body, and my immediate need was to get out of the overturned vehicle. Fright increased when I realized my body was lying in and out of the car. Caked in mud, I slowly stood to my feet and when I did pain ripped through my chest. Gradually, the other five emerged. I heard groans from some and silence from others. We were scared. My first thought was, how could I hide what had just happened? I wonder now if my initial response was similar to Adam and Eve's as they hid, afraid of God, in the garden. We walked through the field, crossed the road and knocked on the door of what I understood later to be a home for student nursing.

An ambulance was called, and we were all taken to the local hospital. I was told two of the boys, one of them being the young man who had switched places to sit on my lap, had sustained injuries that required them both to be flown to a city hospital. A passing taxi driver, who had assessed the accident scene and stopped at the convenience store we never made it to, spread a rumor that some may have passed away. A friend would frantically knock on the door of our home later that day checking to see if I was alive.

After being released from the hospital, an early morning drive home with my parents was marked by silence. Once home, I ran the water in the tub and lowered myself in to wash my hair. I was immediately shocked by the sudden appearance of dirty water, not realizing how much mud I had been covered in. The image of the dirty water had been imprinted in my mind and would be revisited years later in the waters of baptism when I realized how mud-covered I had become. This night was never spoken about with my parents until years later when I shared with my mom what God had spoken to me that night—words spoken to an unchurched, unsaved teenage girl, who didn't know hearing God's voice was possible.

Over the years, I would relive that night, remembering what I used to call "The Voice." For a time, my teenage mind had more questions than answers such as, wouldn't God use bigger words than "OK?" But a larger, private, persistent question would surface over time: "Why me? God, why had you chosen to speak to me?" It would be awhile before love would find its way into my heart as an answer, and I still have one more question about that night for heaven. As I had stood up from the ground, I wonder about the intense pain that ripped through my chest and suddenly went away. I suspect I had received a miracle in the early morning hours of a dark and rainy night, a miracle that healed whatever caused the extreme pain.

Even though I had heard God's voice and our lives were spared, I would become extremely fearful when driving or being driven in inclement weather, particularly in rain or on single-lane dark roads. It wasn't until I was an adult that revelation revealed a thought that would change my thinking. The words God spoke to me as a teenage girl were not just for a moment, but meant for a lifetime— an eternal God speaking a forever love message. No matter what life brings, He says, "You'll be OK."

ENDNOTES

1. 1 John 4:8 (NIV)
2. 1 John 4:19 (NIV)
3. Psalm 139:16-18 (TPT)
4. Jeremiah 29:11 (NIV)
5. Joshua 1:9 (NIV)
6. Isaiah 41:13 (NIV)
7. Philippians 4:8 (NIV)

CHAPTER TWO

ALONE

The day after high school graduation in June of 1990, I moved out of my family home to live with a friend in another city. From an emotional stand point, moving away from home at seventeen wasn't a difficult step for me to take. I had never become too attached to any place we lived and my teenage heart already felt a separation from my family. To be separated geographically would continue to widen the already existing gap.

Barely knowing the basics about budgeting, cleaning, and grocery shopping, my independent spirit would find the way. After moving, the summer was spent working until college began. A few months into the program had me realizing I was not equipped to successfully handle the pace, the workload, the job, and managing life on my own.

Asking for help was never considered, a pattern I established early on. Loneliness set in by the end of the summer as my roommate spent more time with her boyfriend than at home. This aloneness would allow discouragement to keep me company sporadically, and thoughts about myself that had briefly been on hold returned. Procrastinated assignments and unread text books left me scrambling towards the end of the first semester to try and catch up. Even though all was new—the city, home, and friends—old, unhealthy ways of thinking convinced me more than ever of how foolish I was. Every thought magnified as I lay awake late into the night, alone.

Choices

Failure seemed inevitable, and as I felt like I was treading water alone in the ocean, a relationship was rekindled with a man who lived in another city. Unaccountable and independent, I made a significant life decision to drop out of college, pack up, and move yet again to another city, to live with this man. At the age of eighteen, love did not lead, but a desire to be loved did.

I entered into two of the most vulnerable, belittling, degrading years of my life. These two years would heighten once again my already existing insecurity and anxiety. I found myself in a relationship with an angry, verbally abusive man whom I was looking to for love. It wouldn't have mattered if my time spent in this situation had lasted one day or a decade. Every minute of myself I gave to him had been one minute too long.

It was during this period I began to experience symptoms of panic attacks but didn't understand what was happening, or that it even had a name. I would also awaken in the night gasping for breath. When this happened, terror would consume me until a surreal numbness set in. This was the beginning of what I could describe as a teeter-totter ride, feeling fear one day and the absence of feelings the next, in order to survive. The emotional numbness would occur after being exposed to horrific name-calling. Later, I would find myself numbing out in the future whenever I found it necessary to protect myself from hurt feelings, even guarding myself from being disappointed by God. Numbness creates a barrier that does not need to exist between us and our Maker.

Knowing I needed to move on from the situation I was in, I worked two jobs and completed a double diploma as an executive office assistant and legal secretary in the hopes of finding a better paying job that would allow me to move yet again. Many times, my bank balance was zero, and food was sparse. Somehow, I continued to put one foot in front of the other to finish school for a better future. A loss of weight and ongoing stomach upset would put me in front of a doctor more than once, but I never told, never revealing what life was really like.

The day that precipitated the necessary change came when the man I was living with returned home in a drunken, angry state. I watched through the patio window of our apartment as he barreled up the hill towards the building well after midnight. The lamppost light illuminated the danger. An urgency to flee had me bolting from the apartment and down a flight of stairs to hide in the apartment of an acquaintance who lived below. The sound of drawers being dumped from above confirmed it was necessary to stay put. Time seemed to pass slowly as I lay quietly on a bed and stared at the ceiling. Despite being tired and scared, it was a work uniform upstairs in the bedroom closet that was on my mind. I knew I needed to return to the apartment and gather the uniform for my upcoming shift at work that day.

A few hours later, deciding it was quiet enough to return, my landlord unlocked the apartment door to let me in after I told him I had misplaced my key. Slowly, I made my way down the hall towards the bedroom closet to retrieve my uniform. He appeared to have passed out on the bed, but it was the arm that swung out to hit me on the back that moved me to pack my things within the week and walk out the door. Two moves later and a verbal threat instilled in me a long-term fear of being harmed. Unforgiveness, brokenness, and the barrage of humiliating words received during that time would crowd my twenty-year-old heart, even as I closed that door and opened the next.

I don't recall thinking about God at all during those two years, but I do remember a reoccurring phrase that came from within. The words I knew to be true and would whisper to myself were, "This is not who you are." I wanted to find out who I really was. For the girl who thought she was stupid, moving on was the smartest decision she could have made.

Moving On

Within months of leaving, I met my husband during a last minute, late-night visit to a club. We danced, we talked, and we would later joke he was my knight in shining armor who rode in on a white Toyota Tercel. Our dating story isn't one I used to share readily, mostly because of previous decisions I had made and associated with shame. We also didn't really date and knew each other for just under two weeks before moving in together. I know, that's quick. Six months later we were engaged, followed by our wedding nine months after our engagement. Sandwiched in between, we made a significant move, not just from one city to another, but now from one province to another.

Although neither of us were Christians, we felt we were to be married in a church and took the necessary steps for that to happen. These steps included finding a pastor who would agree to marry an unbelieving couple who lived together. The pastor who said yes graciously asked us why we wanted to be married in a church. Our short answer: "We felt we should." At his request, we completed a pre-marriage course and attended two of his church services.

Before dawn on the morning of September 10, 1994, I awoke to a thunderstorm which I would watch from the hotel room I was sharing with my aunt as I contemplated what this important day meant. I was concerned the weather wouldn't turn out, but the blue sky unfolded as we stepped out of the church shortly after saying our "I do's." We were married in a traditional, red carpeted church that I fell in love with at first sight. Tall ceilings, stained glass windows, and a large picturesque cross hung before us, setting the stage for what was to come. We committed to each other, and even though we didn't know it, God did, too.

We celebrated our first anniversary picnic style in the park, eating hot dogs with our now precious baby girl of two months lying on a blanket between us. Simple and sweet. I wondered if others observed our fast-paced relationship as unwise, but God's Spirit had been moving, too. Years later, we would be able to acknowledge that God's presence had tangibly visited us during a moment spent together when we first met, and a second time as we drove into the city limits of our new city, the place we have now called home for twenty-three years.

Family life had begun, and it was almost as if I had been catapulted in an entirely new direction, but this new direction was woven together with the past. Another new city, more new friends, and the breathtaking addition of our baby girl were not enough to completely move on from what came before. It reminds me of the saying, "You can run, but you can't hide." Bouts of a familiar loneliness were trying to steal enjoyment from my time as a new mom, and anxiety frequently knocked at the door of my heart as I held my daughter, vowing that my life experiences would never be hers. I had taken on too much personal responsibility, and a breaking point would soon come.

Increase in More Ways than One

In 1998, I was now twenty-six years old and a mom for the second time with the arrival of another beautiful, very full of life baby girl. We purchased our first home a few months later, a duplex with a decent-sized back yard for our growing family. Dad proudly set up the yard with a swing set, a sandbox and toys. Late nights were spent painting walls and cupboards, personalizing the home we called ours. With no support of family living close by, we were immersed in the routines of raising our children and working diligently to get ahead. Our dream that I would become a full-time stay-at-home mom had also been realized.

All of the increase was good and welcomed. But along with the obvious increase that could be seen, an equally active emotional battle was increasing beneath the surface. I continued to withhold many of my concerns, which produced a constraining, voiceless conversation between me, myself and I.

If you and I had passed each other on the street, or struck up a conversation at the playground while our children played, you might not have perceived that my inner world was in turmoil. I was good at hiding, and hiding comes with a cost. The cost was the inability to go any further than I could take myself and remaining alone in the process.

During this time as anxiety, worry, fears, and fretful thinking would continue to find their place in my day, another challenge came into the mix. Before we could leave the house to go on an outing, everything needed to be clean, orderly, and in its place. My girls were patient in the waiting, and I can picture them playing at the front door while the last dish or toy was put away. Thankfully, they were oblivious to what their mom was going through. They knew the bike ride, walk, or playing at the park was on its way. I recognized I was bordering on obsessive compulsive behavior, and because I recognized what I was doing, I believed I had control over the issue. The truth was I couldn't leave my home without it looking a certain way, so the issue was in control and not me.

Today, I still prefer my home clean and tidy, but I am no longer bound to my preference and can freely leave our home when dishes aren't done or beds are unmade. I had to be intentional for a time. Purposefully not cleaning before going out established a healthier, new "normal" for myself. When we meditate on something excessively, we know that this issue has a hold on us.

Grocery shopping had become a significant source of stress. Wandering the aisles distracted by physical symptoms such as lightheadedness, an upset stomach, and a racing heart would sidetrack me from shopping. For example, a simple task such as bagging a few apples could become so stressful that I would halt the attempt to choose apples as confusion and forgetfulness set in. Feeling overwhelmed became normal. It was devastating as a young woman, to be surrounded by strangers in a public place, struggle to look normal and feel completely alone. Eventually, I would walk in the entrance and immediately leave through the exit, not shopping at all.

Over time, any type of shopping and public place would cause stress and symptoms of anxiety. I didn't like the feelings, so to avoid the feelings I avoided shopping. More and more, I would miss out on opportunities, and in my experience, the more you choose to miss out, the easier it becomes not to go. My bedroom had also become my safe place, and if anxiety or a panic attack occurred while I was out, my only goal was to return home to the safety of my room. Once in my room, I would wait out the feelings until I returned to what I considered normal.

Volunteering at the school had also become a challenge. I found the lights too bright and the bustle of a busy classroom too loud. Self-control would hold back the tears that threatened to flow because of the tremendous guilt I felt for being a broken mom. This was not a healthy way to live, nor was it the life God intended for me.

Stuck in A Moment

Near the end of the year 2000, I agreed to look after a friend's baby in our home upon her return to work. This would seem to be an obvious request to decline, but I really wanted to provide financially and contribute beyond raising my own children. This little one fit into our routine well, and our girls were quite taken by her, except for the occasional jealous outburst from our almost three-year-old.

The days were full, and although I was capable, an irrational fear developed. I became very concerned the baby would somehow be hurt under my care in our home. I felt such an extreme responsibility to keep her safe I became overly cautious tending to her needs. I was so "on" for her during the day, that even as tired as I was, once in bed I switched from worrying about the baby to worrying about my own children. Was I meeting their needs well enough while I cared for the baby?

The pressure I placed on myself was unforgiving and relentless. I considered discontinuing care for the baby but I didn't want to fail and let my friend down. Most days I was exhausted emotionally and physically. A visit to the doctor followed up by blood work revealed my iron levels were too low, which gave me something else to be anxious about. As a family, we ate healthy meals, but to be transparent, I wasn't eating or drinking enough, and proper nutrition combined with a healthy body image matters. The anemia/anxiety combination was aggravating my well-being, and I was about to crash.

At the end of another day caring for my friend's baby, in March of 2001, we said our goodbyes, and upon closing the front door I instantly became aware that I was excessively tired and jittery. I can describe it as an inner shake. I began to pace and told my husband I was going to take a shower. I stepped into the shower, and what happened next seemed to detach me from my mind. My thoughts were no longer my own. Words raced like a train barreling down the tracks with no brakes. I could neither slow down or stop what was happening. I did not have control. Disconnected from myself, I was terrified and certain I was going crazy.

I stepped out of the shower and communicated to my husband I wasn't feeling right. He tried to ask how but unable to explain, an emergency trip to the hospital was made. At the hospital, I was quickly taken to a private room where I would sit with a doctor who asked me questions I no longer remember and could not fully answer. Several hours later, I slowly walked down an empty hospital corridor, sedated, detached, and alone. My husband picked me up in the hospital parking lot with our two girls sleeping in the back seat of our car.

The drug's effect on me was a deep sleep. I woke hours later to an empty house. My husband had taken the girls with him to work. Groggy, dazed, and confused, I sat on the edge of the couch in our living room with my head down. I don't know why, but I remember the way the sun light filtered through the closed sheers on the front window. I was completely unaware of the stereo quietly playing from across the room until suddenly, my ears heard a song: "Oh love, look at you now, you've got yourself stuck in a moment and now you can't get out of it." The song ended with, "It's just a moment this time will pass." I sat alone in that empty room—or was it empty?—and whispered, "God, is that you?"

Determined

My husband purchased the CD by U2, *All That You Can't Leave Behind* so I could listen to the song, "Stuck in a Moment You Can't Get Out Of", as many times as I needed. Armed with a song, an anxiety and phobia workbook that had been suggested, and a few pills from the hospital tucked into my purse for emergency use (which I never used), I was determined, once again, to move on, not comprehending that incomplete healing would be my setback. The stigma of mental illness bothered me, and I wanted the breakdown I was stuck in to go away.

Daily tasks were overwhelming, such as making breakfast for the girls. Anything that included noise or movement such as the television was difficult to tolerate. I committed to participating in crisis counseling at the hospital. Doctor's visits were frequent, and a decision was made about the use of an antidepressant. I chose not to. I wasn't comfortable with the decision to take an antidepressant and was determined to get better on my own, whatever "on my own" meant. During an appointment with my family doctor, he casually asked, "Do you have a church family?" I remember thinking, "I'm crazy, what does church have to do with this?" That annoying question was a seed planted that would grow in a few short years.

My incredible husband (and he really is) was keeping the house together, and I was doing what I could to keep myself together. My diagnosis during this time was "generalized anxiety disorder," but I was surprisingly determined not to be labelled, because I didn't want it. If only I had been this determined in other areas of my life. All I knew is that I was perpetually nervous, and full-blown panic attacks were frequent. There seemed to be no rules or bargaining with my body. Some days I struggled to breathe, and other days placing one foot in front of the other looked like success. The song gave me hope, and the workbook gave me context. Reading about this illness brought temporary comfort, with the list of symptoms I knew all too well. Vocabulary such as "fight or flight" allowed me to realize others out there were familiar with what I was going through.

Two weeks after my crisis, we drove to join extended family in another city for Easter dinner. The drive was difficult, and I wanted the car to turn around more than once to take me home. Our girls were excited, dressed up for the occasion, and I am again thankful for their innocence of the distress their mom was in. We walked into the home we were visiting, and I immediately went to sit alone in a back bedroom—too many people, too much talking and too much going on. I was numb. I don't know how long I sat on the bed in the back bedroom, until suddenly, I heard and felt a zap in my brain that sounded like electricity. I knew a wire had been reconnected—another "suddenly" from the God who continued to help me even when I wasn't asking.

Hiding

The reconnection I felt brought improvement, and I no longer felt crazy. A friend unaware of my struggles, came to our door asking if I could help her out and watch her daughter. I let her know I wasn't feeling well, that I was struggling emotionally and wouldn't be able to help this time. Her response strengthened an already formed belief. She looked at me and said, "You look fine." I heard "I don't believe you."

For over a decade, I would battle with the lie of not being believed, and this would stop me from sharing with my doctor and future psychologist how I was really doing. I would divulge enough, but not too much. As a young girl, I hid my fears and heartbreak. As a teenager, I hid behind being quiet; as a young adult, I hid behind pain; and now, as a young woman, I hid behind unbelief. I lived with a pattern of hiddenness that was hurting me.

I learned to offer what I thought other people wanted to hear and gave the right answers instead of the real answers. My hiddenness was determined by me, to reveal what I thought you would accept and like. I didn't know I could hide in the shadow of His wings or in the cleft of the rock. Being hidden in Christ would eventually save me, but even when change came, I would continue the pattern by hiding God's active truth that was without a doubt impacting my life. I held back from others all He had done for me, including supernatural experiences, and kept my testimony locked up in a thankful heart, all because I thought I wouldn't be believed. Now, I desire my conversations to be about noticing Him in every situation.

Years of hiding worry and unresolved wounds was dominating my life. The truth was, I was scared, and although I had a husband who would do anything for me, beautiful children, and a home, I could not shake feeling broken and alone. I was eager for this time to pass, as the words of the song sung. It would come to an end, but not the way I had expected, and the God who loved me would not pass me by.

CHAPTER THREE
TRUST

Up to this point, I continued to look primarily to myself for answers and my healing, although "healing" was not a word I would have used at the time. Controlling myself and "drifting" were happening simultaneously. The control meant, "me trying to fix me," and pretending I was doing better than I was. When that became tiring, I would drift, which meant spending some days just getting by instead of thriving.

I didn't always trust the future, so I worried about it, and maybe if I worried about it, something bad wouldn't happen—or at the very least, if it did happen, I would be better prepared and better able to cope with it. That was confusing to write about—no wonder I felt confused most days!

Have you ever heard yourself or someone else start a sentence with, "What IF?", finishing it with a doom and gloom outcome? We can become so conditioned to living lopsided and not even realize we are. I certainly was, and it's a life-draining way to live.

What IF...... life could be lived differently?

Trust is defined as the, "assured reliance on the character, ability, strength, or truth of someone or something."

The "What IF?" life I was living was closer to becoming introduced to Jesus who asked questions too.

"Do you believe that I am able to do this?"[1]
"Who do you say I am?"[2]
"Why are you so afraid?"[3]
"Why are you thinking these things in your [heart]?"[4]

My mind hadn't been the only part of my body to experience a break. On January 21, 2000, one year prior to the breakdown, I accidently fractured my left ankle. I automatically trusted my ankle would heal. That wasn't difficult for me to believe. However, I didn't have the same trust with regards to the healing of my mind.

Broken Bone Versus a Broken Mind

On a typical cold winter's morning, a neighbor suggested an early morning skate at our community out door ice rink. Thinking this could be a fun way to spend the morning with the girls, we bundled up and made our way to the rink. The rink was quiet, only the sounds of our blades moving across the ice or the tires of an occasional vehicle passing by on the snow and ice covered side street could be heard.

I had finished pushing my youngest daughter in an umbrella stroller across the ice of the upper skating rink and was making our way back to the lower rink. Crossing hard packed snow, I was steps away from the lower rink when the blade of my left skate became caught in an already formed blade mark in the snow. On that quiet, wintery morning I now heard another kind of sound in my ears. A crack, followed by a pregnant pause and keen awareness that my ankle was broken. I couldn't immediately find my voice, only a whispered help as I called out to my friend.

A wave of nausea hit my stomach as I lowered myself to the ground to quickly but carefully remove my skate. Swelling was immediate, along with a call for help sending an ambulance on its way and my husband arriving soon after. Two young ambulance attendants carried me up an incline, to the waiting ambulance and a conversation ensued as they decided how to carefully protect my now grotesque ankle for the ride.

A broken ankle meant worry. I declined the pain medication they offered me and despite my condition, was more concerned about reminding the attendants how to drive on winter road conditions. I even requested they not speed and suggested lights weren't necessary as I wanted to arrive safely at the hospital. They probably wanted to give me more than pain medication that day.

Safely at the hospital, I had my foot x-rayed and when three faces appeared at the window of the x-ray department, stretching their necks forward to get a close look at my foot, I knew the results weren't in my favor. After receiving the news that my ankle had multiple breaks, the doctor suggested surgery. I of course, disagreed. The thought of surgery terrified me. After discussing the options, our final decision resulted in a temporary boot cast, followed by trips back and forth to the hospital during the first few days to assess the swelling and potential bone movement. Each trip was an event. Imagine a slippery front side walk to conquer, a small car to be comfortably seated in, winter weather driving, anxious me and a still patient husband escorting me back and forth to the hospital. At the end of the few days swelling had decreased; no bones had shifted and a permanent cast was in place for six weeks.

I knew I needed a break but this was not the break I imagined. Laying on the couch that first night, uncomfortable and in pain, I stared up at the ceiling and grumpily asked, "What do you want?" If I had heard Him that night, maybe His answer would have been, "You."

In the weeks ahead, we received intermittent help in our home. A new definition of vulnerability, was my mother in law washing my hair in a bucket while I lay on the living room floor. Nearing the end of the six weeks, two young Mormon men knocked on our front door. I answered, adorned with crutches and my girls each gripping a leg. They immediately offered to wash dishes, along with anything else to be done. I admit, I was tempted by the two sincere strangers standing at my door eager to help.

The white cast had announced a broken bone, just as a white flag announces surrender. My injured ankle was visible, drawing compassion from strangers and friends alike. Unable to be hidden or ignored. A brokenness that is easily accepted and understood. A broken mind for the most part is invisible, can sometimes be hidden, rejected and misunderstood. The commonalities, both resulted in sleepless nights, were painful, unplanned and in need of healing. Both had needed emergency care, follow up and a plan for progress.

I trusted that my body would do what it needed to do to mend the broken bones. When my mind broke, I lost trust in me. An x-ray visibly confirmed my broken ankle and an x-ray confirmed when it was healed. No one could x-ray my mind and confirm when I was better. It was obvious, my ankle needed rest to heal. Attempting to walk on my broken ankle, would never have been considered, yet I needed to walk with a broken mind. Rest didn't seem to be as justified and I didn't know how to rest my mind as needed.

When the time came for the cast removal, it was difficult to imagine stepping on my foot with its loss of motion, attached to a leg with loss of muscle. Building the strength and confidence to walk again, began by walking with two crutches to none, walking in a swimming pool, physio therapy, strolls on the sidewalk and in time conquering our neighborhood hill. The first couple of weeks after the cast was removed my ankle looked angry, red and swollen as it rebelled from being used.

A common comment from people seeing the cast off for the first time was, "That's wonderful, you're better." How quick we can be to assume with our eyes that see. The part unseen was the rehab and walking the hill those first few times, crying because I wanted to quit from the pain. No one else could walk for me. I had to do it.

My mind was also in need of rehabilitation, had also suffered loss of motion and occasionally rebelled from use. My mental health needed to continue to improve and although I was slowly attempting to climb a figurative hill, there would be another mountain to conquer before true turn around would happen. This would also include hard work and a lot of tears but just as my foot was able to bare weight once again, in time so would my mind.

Subtle Change

We became pregnant near the end of 2001 with my gorgeous, sweet baby boy. I had visited my doctor beforehand asking his opinion about my well-being to handle another baby and he was not concerned. I didn't completely trust my emotions to handle a third pregnancy due to current struggles but each time I read bed time stories to my two girls, I pictured reading to three. It's one thing to lose trust in others but when you begin to lose trust in yourself and don't have faith, where does that leave you? It left me, struggling to get by.

We were excited to be pregnant, until nine weeks into the pregnancy I experienced a bit of a complication and a matter of fact practitioner, not my family doctor, told me I'd probably lost the pregnancy. Through an ultrasound, we discovered I hadn't lost our baby, but the experience was the catalyst to allowing fear to dominate throughout the pregnancy. With an absence of trust for a positive outcome, I tried to lean on myself, once again, to handle my feelings. How I wish, I had reached out for support during this time.

As the pregnancy progressed, I would find myself flipping through the radio stations on the stereo. The same stereo that had played U2's song one year earlier. I was flipping through the stations because I no longer wanted to listen to top twenty countdowns or rock music, so I settled on a soft rock station playing golden oldies like my parents had listened to. I recognized I was searching but didn't know for what. This change also showed up at our dinner table. Before eating our dinner one evening, I suggested to my husband we could each take turns around the table to share one thing we were thankful for before we ate. God was setting us up, subtly getting us ready to be introduced not only to Him but worship music and prayer.

As the end of the pregnancy drew near, a move to a new home was fast approaching. A friend suggested while I was nine months pregnant and packing that the Vacation Bible School, held at the nearby Lutheran Church would be a great half day option for our girls to attend while my hands were full. It was also added on that it was cheap. This cheap option came with questions such as, "What was a Vacation Bible School?" and "What would they teach?"

We decided our girls could attend and at the end of Vacation Bible Camp, day one, I stood uncomfortably in the foyer of the church waiting for their time to finish. The leader ended the morning in the sanctuary with the children, closing with these words:

> "Trust in the Lord with all your heart
> And lean not on your own understanding;
> In all your ways submit to him,
> And he will make your paths straight."[5]

The words had my attention, but not my affection. Irritated, I couldn't figure out how you were to not lean on your own understanding. All I had known for thirty years was to lean on my understanding for every decision, every worry, parenting, marriage, finances, relationships, and the list could go on.

But in the eyes of my two children, day one had been an absolute success. They were excited; I was marginally unimpressed. Not only were they looking forward to day two but they were now armed with new music. The new sound I had been searching for on the radio was in my daughters' hands, and I didn't know it. Space was found for the girls to listen to their new CD on the landing of our basement staircase—one of the only spaces left without a packed box. We played the CD on repeat, and both the girls and I enjoyed it. God had used music once again, and I can only imagine how heaven celebrated as worship music was welcomed into our home.

The VBS week wrapped up, and our girls had a request, one that would become relentless. They repeatedly asked, "When can we go back there?" "Back there" meant back to church and back to the place where I'd heard about trust. After moving, and the birth of our very loved baby boy in August of 2002, we explained to the girls that we would visit church after Christmas. This was an intentional decision to bypass a season we knew was significant but understood little about.

The Invitation

We were true to our word. The first Sunday of January, 2003, our young family walked through the doors of our first church. We met up with a family from the neighborhood we knew. An invitation had been extended to us previously by this family, but just like my doctor, who had asked two years earlier about having a church family, it was an ask that didn't fully stick. We were warmly welcomed to church and nervously took our seats. Out of everything that took place that morning, it was the offering plate I remembered. We scrounged for change as I processed the twenty dollar bills and envelopes stacked in the offering plate that passed by. Slowly, God was revealing to us those things He cared about such as thankfulness, music, trust, and now generosity.

We returned the following Sunday, and during the service, it was announced that Alpha, a ten-week course introducing the Christian faith was being offered. I signed up. We decided I would attend first, and my husband would stay home with the children. When the first night of Alpha commenced, I found myself seated with a group of people around a table at the church, eating a meal prepared for us. The group was casually talking about church experiences as they ate. I was unchurched and unable to relate to the conversation around the table. I burst into tears and asked, "What about God?"—the first of many questions that would surface in this new season.

Each week, I looked forward to attending the meeting, and within a couple of weeks, I really wanted a Bible. After inquiring, I was directed to a Christian bookstore close to home. My heart was racing when I entered the book store, certain everyone could see I didn't know what I was doing. A kind young lady led me to a section of Bibles. More questions, "Why were there so many Bibles to choose from?" and "What were translations?" She handed me a black, leather, New International Version Bible with maps. Paying at the counter, I was amused by the fact that this was the most expensive book I had ever purchased. Surprised by the price, but deeply proud of my purchase, I was excited to show my husband.

Sitting up in bed that night, I planned on reading my new Bible. I had loved reading from an early age. True stories have always been my favorite, intrigued by tragedy turned triumph scenarios. I was captivated by tales of overcoming, good versus evil and redemptive endings. However, reading this true story came with legitimate concerns: "How would I read the entire Bible quickly and understand?" This book on my lap, containing the answers to living well, would become another silent stressor—more to achieve with the possibility of more failure.

My way of being—the worry, anxiety, control, and beliefs— would be challenged by this book of love sitting on my lap. Flipping to page one, as I had at the age of ten when I had been given a red New Testament at school, I began with the words, "In the beginning…" The ten-year-old girl filled with every intention to read this book had only been able to read a few pages before giving up. This time, I wouldn't always find it easy, but I wouldn't give up.

As the Alpha weeks continued to pass, I looked forward to connecting with the group, but found myself not always connecting with the weekly videos. Information seemed to go over my head, and I was unable to easily retain what I was hearing. Approximately half-way through the course, it was time for the Holy Spirit weekend retreat. Distrust filled me as the weekend approached, and I read ahead in our hand-out. I was determined not to be tricked or manipulated into a decision I didn't want to make. This sudden attitude, I believe, may have been partially driven by the spiritual battle taking place over my life.

After arriving at the hotel with another couple, I noticed extra volunteers in attendance. This quickly threw me off, and my mood became a mess. My mind was rattled with a "me versus them" scenario. By the afternoon, we watched the video introducing us to the Holy Spirit, and when the video ended we were invited to take an opportunity to pray with someone. I assessed the room, saw someone familiar, and told God, "I will only pray with that woman." "That woman" was now closing the blinds, and we had been getting to know each other slowly during this time. Lowering my head again, within moments I heard movement in front of me. She had pulled up a chair and now sat facing me.

Head down and battling self-consciousness, the desire to hide coursed through my veins. Having not prayed with anyone before, she gently and skillfully led, asking me first to confess my sins. Shocked, I totally didn't know how to answer. The word sin eluded me. How was I sinful? Wasn't that a word reserved for murderers and thieves? Eventually, I answered with an apology for not always treating my husband kindly. She continued to pray, "Lord, forgive her for everything spoken and unspoken." Her words etched in my mind, my thoughts spun—what had I forgotten to say? After that, she asked if I wanted to receive Jesus? I did. I didn't know why and wasn't even sure I entirely believed in Jesus, but I went ahead anyway.

I repeated her prayer, and at the age of 30, life as I knew it would change. An unfamiliar sensation permeated my being. I was in a zone wavering between extreme self-consciousness and elation. Unaware of any time that had passed, I opened my eyes, surprised to find we were the only ones left in the room. Slightly confused by the fact we were alone because I had been certain someone had been standing beside us the entire time, I asked my prayer partner if someone had been with us? She answered not with words, but with a smile. I know now who stood with us that day—the man who I had invited into my heart, Jesus.

Heart Awareness

Walking from the meeting room to the elevator, I was convinced my heart was wide open, exposed for all to see. What I sensed seemed unusually exaggerated, and as I stepped into the occupied elevator, the openness I was encountering, although exhilarating, alarmed me in the presence of people. Throughout the remainder of the evening and into the morning, a slow, semi-conscious decision took place to close the door to my heart that had been swung wide open. During our final session, a leader called me out in front of the group: "Is there anything you want to share?"

The leadership had probably celebrated my decision, but I didn't know how to celebrate my yes and was offended to be put on the spot. I didn't share that morning, but I would learn that what God had opened would not be closed, as hard as I might try. The Lord had encountered me and opened my heart as a gift, which I would learn more about in time.

During the ride home, I knew I was different but didn't have the language to articulate the feeling. For the better part of my life, my feelings had determined my mood and my outlook on life. My relationship with my feelings was along the same lines of the relationship I had with fear. Both were easily influenced by negative thinking.

When we started going to church, I had extraordinary feelings that I was unable to express with language because the language I was learning was new—words like presence, glory, and even peace. In our church journey, the message I sometimes received was that feelings were wrong. Yet I could feel God's presence, His healing, His compassion, and His power. I could feel people's hearts at times, or the atmosphere of a room. My feelings, up to this point, had been used to minimize my life, but God wanted to show me the benefits of feeling.

My heart had been recalibrated, and without a frame of reference for the magnitude of what I had said yes to, I returned home wondering what this would mean for myself and my family. The first morning home after the Alpha weekend, I leaned against the glass of our kitchen patio door and gazed up at the sky, feeling as if I were discovering it for the first time, and strangely, I was. The stars of old still hung in the sky, and heaven had a plan to unfold.

In a few years, I would have a vision of my heart. In this vision, I could see Jesus lying in my heart as though resting in a hammock, hands propped behind His head. He was completely relaxed and at ease. He was loving my heart to life.

"Come to me, all you who are weary and burdened, and I will give you rest. Take my yoke upon you and learn from me, for I am gentle and humble in heart, and you will find rest for your souls. For my yoke is easy and my burden is light."[6]

ENDNOTES

1. Matthew 9:28 (NIV)
2. Matthew 16:15 (NIV)
3. Mark 4:40 (NIV)
4. Luke 5:22 (NIV)
5. Proverbs 3:5-6 (NIV)
6. Matthew 11:28-30 (NIV)

CHAPTER 4
MIRACLE IN A MOMENT

Sunday morning became the highlight of my week, and our family quickly became regular church attenders. God was what my life had been missing. The existence of a "church family" my doctor had asked about was beginning to make sense, and the substantial desire to be at church was a gift. I did become concerned one morning when I realized I was thinking about God a lot and wondered if I was focused on Him too much. The concern was quickly dispelled.

To learn more about God became an insatiable hunger as I bought, borrowed, and signed out as many books as I had time to read and attempt to retain. This was the beginning of filling the empty, barren part of myself that only He could fill. I would grieve the years I felt I had lived life without Him, initially wondering how much I had missed out, not yet realizing God would make up for lost time.

We experienced many firsts at church that year, which included taking communion. That day is etched into my memory as I remember nervously walking to the front to receive communion for the first time. It felt personal when the words, "His body broken for you," and "His blood shed for you," were spoken to me. By this point we had read and heard teachings regarding the cross, but Jesus seemed to be a man I couldn't grasp, and to not grasp Jesus as a Christian didn't seem like something I should share.

I may not have been able to grasp Jesus early on, but in the next year I grew in the gifts of the Spirit and developed an ease with the Holy Spirit. The beautiful part of this was a child-like nature that characterized these early days of growth. I would prophesy and not know that's what had happened, or would receive a word of knowledge and not realize it had a name. The simplicity and ease made it all seem normal and fun. I hadn't yet been taught through a class or sermon but was being trained by God himself.

Another crisis was on its way, but the God of miracles, in a moment, would visit me with needed change.

Encountering Strength

On the morning of Saturday, April 24, 2004, I took a seat near the back of our church, trying to decide whether I would stay for the planned women's event. Feeling not quite myself, I sensed darkness lingering close by. We had now been attending church for over a year, and in recent months, I had encountered evil a few times in our home. I continued to read my Bible, but was finding it increasingly difficult to do so. Uncertain whether I would be believed, I kept the evil encounters to myself.

Deciding to stay at the event, a few of us made plans to go out for lunch after the morning session. During lunch I was distracted, unfocused, and had trouble being social. I looked out the window of the restaurant and became concerned when I noticed that the nearby store signs appeared magnified. The letters loomed, and by the time we headed back to the church, I was quietly deep-breathing, trying to fend off the impending panic attack.

We returned to the event, and darkness continued to press in around the property line of my mind. A tug of war was battling for my fate. Having wrestled long enough, the need to leave became urgent, and my fate was sealed during the five-minute ride home. For the second time, my mind was not entirely my own, and the thief who had taunted and not left me alone was trying to steal, kill and destroy once again. But Jesus said that He came so we may have life.[1]

Retreating to our bedroom for safety, I hoped that maybe I could regain control with deep breaths and some space. However, I couldn't even look at the tree outside our window and watch the branches blowing in the wind. My mind yelled at me not to look, and it was like being frozen in a state I was unable to escape from.

Monday morning arrived, and my husband stood at the threshold of our front door, desperately trying to convince me to leave for a doctor's appointment. I didn't want to leave, and for the first time, found myself unable to leave. My feet wouldn't leave the security of our home, and in that moment, it was as if all color had left my world.

My husband wouldn't give into the fear that had me paralyzed and refused to take "no" for an answer. Eventually, I followed, sat in the passenger seat of our vehicle, and slouched low to endure the drive. My senses were overwhelmed and further challenged by oncoming traffic and sounds. The movement of life was rushing towards and around me, boxing me into a space I didn't belong in but couldn't get out of.

I fixated on a man riding his bike in our lane and felt a sudden surge of anger. How could this man riding his bike just carry on with his day? Where was he headed as I suffered? He was free, and I was not. If this was how I would live the rest of my life, I didn't want it. It felt like torture and an unbearable way to live.

This time I would leave the doctor's office with a prescription. He had some legitimate concerns regarding my mental health, and the anxiety was severe. I coped from one minute to the next, unable to pray or read.

After a few days, I somehow drove the three-minute drive to our neighborhood pharmacy to fill the prescription I really didn't want to take. The shelves in the store closed in on me as I waited. With a small white paper bag in my hand, I returned to our vehicle to drive home. Driving home, I was about to signal left to enter a left-hand turn lane, when my plans were "suddenly" interrupted by His voice. "Go to the church." I already thought I had gone crazy again, so momentarily arguing with God in my broken state didn't seem so out of touch. I didn't want to go to the church. I didn't want anyone else to know my circumstances, but even in brokenness, I was able to hear and follow His voice. Instead of turning left, I drove through the lights, took the next right, and ended up in the church parking lot. Attempting to bargain with God, I told Him I would do a drive-through, entering and exiting just as I had many times at the grocery store.

As it turned out, I didn't leave, because out of my right eye, I glimpsed the young son of the woman who had prayed the salvation prayer with me during the Alpha Holy Spirit weekend. She had become like a mentor during those first couple of years and was aware I was unwell. She inquired why I was there, I didn't know why. I followed her through the front doors of the church and across the foyer to a small library.

We sat face to face, once again to pray. One year after I had been introduced to Jesus as Savior, I would now be introduced to Him as Healer. I don't remember the words she prayed that day, but when she'd finished, she did ask if I had seen anything. Yes, I had, and how did she know? I shared that I had seen the backside of an eagle sitting high on a pole with its head turned over its shoulder, eyes looking directly at me. The eagle looked strong, and I was not. This would be my first vision, and not forgotten.

I walked out the front doors of the church after the encounter and noticed the sky no longer felt like it was sitting on my head. I left with a measure of strength I hadn't had when I drove into the parking lot.

The following day, I nervously swallowed one pill from my prescription after making the decision to try. After taking the pill, I noticed myself behaving oddly, and the panic attacks hours after taking the pill resumed with a vengeance. I returned to my doctor's office with a firm decision that taking a pill wasn't for me. This time, I left with a verbal prescription. The instruction was to take on minimal responsibility, share my thoughts with my husband, and allow my mind time to heal. I was also referred to a registered Christian psychologist. I committed to the appointments and am thankful for the care received. God partnered with this woman during my time spent in her care, and I always left better than when I walked in. Even today, I wouldn't hesitate to return if I felt the need.

We had three small children, but my husband was more than willing to do what was required. Finances, shopping (which I was unable to complete anyway), most of the cooking, and decision making would be his. Sometimes terrifying thoughts plagued my mind, which I never did communicate, but I did begin to share more than I had before, and he was able to handle it.

Shortly after this breakdown, my husband was planning an event to be hosted in a local art gallery. He asked repeatedly if I would join him for a tour of the venue. This was not an easy outing, but I wanted to support him. We weren't in the gallery long before I found myself standing before a painting mostly painted in black. It was dark and disturbing, and evil creatures looked back at me from the canvas. I quickly turned away from that painting and took only a few steps before standing in front of another large painting that couldn't have been more different from the first. The blue sky, white clouds and a woman lying on her back in a canoe with outstretched arms captivated me. I didn't have well-articulated words but that woman had my attention. I turned to my husband and said, "I want to be like her."

© Joseph Cross (used with permission)
www.josephcrossart.com

Just as a song had given me hope, and a vision strength, this painting forecasted the possibility of a future, at peace and free. Months later, as an early Christmas present, my husband purchased a giclee of the appropriately named painting, "Happy Feet, Happy Mind," and it continues to hang in our home today. Every so often, I'll find myself staring at the picture, reflecting on how far I've come, no longer overwhelmed by fear but instead by God's goodness. Peace and freedom are no longer a distant longing. Today, I am more like that woman, arms wide open as I continue to look towards the sky.

Spring turned to summer and God continued to point me towards beauty. A friend would take me on frequent, much-needed walks. An avid gardener, she would point out flowers and trees along the way. At first I looked but wasn't really interested or inspired by the beauty of creation she could see. That summer, she generously created flowerbeds in our yard and transplanted plants as a gift from her garden to ours. God in His wisdom gave me a reason to go outside, encouraging the color to come back into my world.

Power of Serving

The commitment to Sundays and serving became an extraordinary channel to receiving a miracle. When I didn't want to show up to church, the commitment to serve kept me going, and my ability to serve increased, even when taken on from a place of fear. What was even more incredible, was the ability to function well on a Sunday when I was unable to enter the grocery store nearby.

The offering plates that caught my attention on our first day of church were now in my hands to pass down the rows, and the greeter at the front door who had warmly welcomed us had left such a positive, lasting impression, I was now following in his footsteps. Even in brokenness, serving others can become a gateway to falling further in love with God and His church.

Transitioning into fall would not only bring weather changes, but a supernatural transition as well. A leader approached me with the invitation to lead a mom's bible study. I was shocked by the invitation, never having attended a mom's study before, let alone lead one. What if they really knew me? I also asked myself the entrapping question so many of us entertain: "Am I qualified?" What I didn't see in myself was recognized by another. What I didn't believe about myself, someone else believed in, and that can be a catalyst to bravery and stepping out.

I said yes, and the book for the study was placed into my hands. The evening before the study was to begin, I thought it might be a good idea to prepare. Once the kids were tucked into bed, I sat alone in our living room, lights dimmed, and opened to the first lesson. I turned to page one and direction was given to read a few verses from a psalm, a cool shiver ran down both my arms. I knew God was asking for my attention. I spoke out loud, "You must really want me to read this," and slowly I read these words that leapt off the page and into my heart:

> "Praise the Lord, my soul;
> all my inmost being, praise his holy name.
> Praise the Lord, my soul,
> and forget not all his benefits,
> who forgives all your sins
> and heals all your diseases,
> who redeems your life from the pit
> and crowns you with love and compassion,
> who satisfies your desires with good things
> so that your youth is renewed
> like the eagle's."[2]

When I read the verse, especially the words "and heals all your diseases" I received a miracle in that moment. I knew the panic attacks were finished, and the breakdowns were done. I would walk it out tentatively, but I knew, and no one could have convinced me otherwise. I also had no idea eagles were in the Bible. Stunned, the vision from six months earlier flashed before my eyes as the dots connected. I didn't know yet what it meant to "Praise the Lord, my soul", the words uncomfortable as I read them but I did know that God could change everything in a moment.

This was an amazing way to begin leading the mom's group, and as that opportunity finished, a new one was offered. That Christmas, we were invited to a gathering at the youth pastor's home. Sitting on their living room floor, I conversed with one of the worship leaders. Another shocking request came as he invited me to sing on the worship team. Looking at him, I brought up the fact he didn't even know if I could sing. This was followed by silence and a shrug of his shoulders. A few days later, a reminder message was left on my answering machine to attend practice. I was privileged to serve alongside this team of faithful, mature men and women for nine months.

Not one Sunday passed that I didn't stand on the platform scared and self-conscious. Not only had God brought His sound into our stairwell two years earlier, but now I was singing His sound in His church. I fondly remember when our worship leader turned to me during our Good Friday service in 2005, asking me to lead out by myself on the next song. One year earlier I had been unable to leave my home, and now I had received a miracle, led a mom's Bible study, and would now sing in front of a few hundred people. Serving is powerful.

Depression

I was no longer trapped on the mouse wheel of panic and anxiety attacks. However, my mind was now quiet enough to hear my heart which revealed the depression underneath. I spent the next several years moving in and out of varying degrees of this depression that had existed undercover, masked by the noise of anxiety. It would invite me, now more than ever, to settle into its boring existence.

Some days were long and drawn out as I lounged effortlessly on the couch in tears. Hopelessness came from time to time, and the pit became a place to overcome. Loneliness was an unforgiving lie with a plan to consume me like an unquenchable thirst. Emotional instability was opportunistic. I've never bungee jumped and don't plan on it anytime soon, but I imagine my emotions as a person hanging off the end of the bungee rope, bouncing around after a jump. Too many days, I would find myself at the end of my rope, in desperate need of stability.

From experience, depression magnifies the ability to feel sorry for one's self, never urging you to go anywhere or leaving you alone long enough to care. As hours and days pass, you soon can find yourself realizing that life continues whether you're on the couch or off.

On April 22, 2007, I wrote a list of the top ten things I wanted most in life at that time. This was number two:

- To not feel lonely, but confident and satisfied by me and Jesus.

This want has been realized. Being alone no longer feels lonely and Jesus is enough.

I imagine now that Jesus was most likely reclining in the chair across from my couch during those days spent in depression. He was waiting as I waited, listening as I wept, and interceding for me as I slept. There were two truths present in the room, mine and His. His truth would win.

Perseverance

Perseverance is defined as the "continued effort to do or achieve something despite difficulties, failure, or opposition."

Perseverance provides momentum to keep going and fuels the desire to continue to dream. How many times have you read a book or watched a movie, hanging on to know how it will end? How is this going to turn out? Perseverance kept me going. Deep down, I wanted to know how my life would turn out.

I persevered in reading the Bible when my memory lagged and not a lot made sense because the Word I read became living and active inside of me. I would persevere in prayer when I didn't hear, when I was afraid to ask or afraid of the answer, and when answers didn't seem to come. I persevered in worship even when I didn't feel like praising and found it hard to engage.

Perseverance included standing before God, weeping when I felt misunderstood or rejected and continuing to do so until my perspective changed. The change included looking towards heaven and confidently stating to God, "I know that you know." Knowing that he knew became my go to. When others don't or won't understand, He does. Taking my eyes off people and fixing them on Him was important. Perseverance meant I wasn't just looking at the coat lying with me on the couch as I cried but I was making the effort to put it on and do up all the buttons, to wear the Lord Jesus Christ.[3]

There were distinct times when I would picture a safe and hear the spin and click of the combination. It was God's way of showing me I was on track, that I had progressed, and as the combinations continued to click, I would find myself having more good days than bad.

When asked how I healed from depression, I can confidently say, "I sought God, or at the very least, thought about God on good days as well as difficult days, and I showed up. I would go to God's House when I didn't feel like it, when I didn't want to, when I didn't understand, and even when I didn't like being there."

"Blessed is the one who perseveres under trial because, having stood the test, that person will receive the crown of life that the Lord has promised to those who love him."[4]

ENDNOTES

1. John 10:10 (NIV)
2. Psalm 103:1-5 (NIV)
3. Romans 13:14 (NIV)
4. James 1:12 (NIV)

CHAPTER FIVE
THE ALTAR

I carry a deep respect for the area of the church that is recognized as the altar, or the front. Significant healing has taken place when I have approached and stood in the altar. Early on in our church journey, I sensed the front of the room was more than a platform, but a place set apart to magnify the Lord and be on earth as it is heaven.

I'm not limiting where and how God heals, but the altar is a powerful place. I am thankful for the men and women who have faithfully served to establish and build the local churches that God has invited our family to be a part of. My life has flourished in His courts and needed this place. "Better is one day in your courts than a thousand elsewhere."[1]

I've observed men and women approach the altar with expectation and reluctance. I've stood at the front uncertain, and kneeled and wept. I've laid face down, shouted (which has been a stretch), jumped, and danced. Other times I have approached the front with fear and anticipation, feeling vulnerable, alone, and part of the crowd, but ultimately, it's been a place where I have gotten over myself because God is there.

We can view the church as flawed or see the church as the bride Jesus is coming back for, without spot or wrinkle.[2] For all He's done for me, it would be a mistake to take the time I've been given to complain.

Much in a church can change, but what doesn't change is the God who has invited you and me to step forward, participate in a divine exchange, and be altered at the altar.

The following are a few of my divine exchanges at the altar and the stories that followed:

Baptism

At the age of seven months, my parents, who didn't attend church, chose to have me christened in an Anglican Church. I know with all my heart that God has honored the decision my parents made on behalf of my life.

When we started attending church in 2003, it quickly became important to us to baptize our children as explained in the Lutheran Church we were attending. Despite the terminology differences and degrees of belief around how and what takes place, I believe we dedicated our children to the Lord and were led by Him to do so. We wanted to acknowledge they were His, and that we needed His help to parent them.

When we baptized our children in the altar, I asked the pastor if I could be baptized also. I was eager to give God everything and did not understand the differences between denominations at the time. He asked if I had been baptized before? I communicated I had been christened. His answer was, no. He was clear in stating that God did not make a mistake the first time. I don't think God made a mistake either, but I knew I was being led, longing for change I could not define. I may not have been baptized on that day, but we were excited to present our children and felt we were making the right decision at the right time.

We spent two and half years receiving a good foundation from our first church, and during my final weeks on the worship team we sang a new song, "The River" by Brian Doerksen. I would listen to the song on repeat and knew God was leading me to be baptized.

In the fall of 2005, we transitioned to what would be considered a more charismatic church. After eight months of attending, it was announced that baptisms would be held. I could hardly wait.

On Sunday, June 11, 2006, my husband and I were baptized, fully immersed in a portable hot tub set up on the platform. Friends and family joined us to share and celebrate our decision. The friend who had prayed with me the day I was saved and in the library of the Lutheran Church when I was unwell, now stood on my right supporting me in prayer once again.

Our pastor stood with me in the tub, and had started to speak, but stopped, distracted by a noise he thought was being caused by the tub. It took a few moments to realize it was not the tub but the sound of a heavy rain hitting the roof of the church. It was not unlike the sound of rain that hit the windshield of the car I rode in as a teenager girl, but instead of leaning back into a dirty tub of water as I had many years before, I was about to lean back into life. I heard my friend say, "It's healing rain." My pastor dunked me under.

As my pastor drew me back to the bottom of the tub, I was surprised by a single thought, which was, "I wish I could stay here." The part of me that wanted to stay hidden would be forced to reemerge, and as I reemerged, the rain stopped. It was immediate and did not go unnoticed.

Later we were told someone had checked outside during the downpour and observed only one cloud in the sky that morning, located directly above the church.

Visitation

On Sunday, December 3, 2006, I felt low. I don't remember a trigger or an event leading up to how I felt that day—I just did. The Sunday service ended, and wanting to be home, I quickly headed towards the sanctuary doors to leave. Stopping at the doors, I looked back at the altar for a moment and wrestled with the idea that maybe I should turn back and ask for prayer. Up to this point, this was not something I had yet done. After some time of wavering, I turned once again to leave the room but was stopped as Holy Spirit whispered to go back.

I walked towards the altar, my legs moving almost without me. I stood in front of my pastor and said, "I don't want to be here anymore." These are not words most people are prepared to hear, but the Holy Spirit in my pastor was. Almost as if it was a sign, I watched the blue of his eyes change in an instant, and an edge appeared that wasn't previously there. A switch had been turned on in the Spirit. I closed my eyes, and he prayed. I wouldn't remember any of the words, until another "suddenly" moment, when it seemed my ears opened just as he was praying who I was in God's eyes and confirming how I had been called.

By this time a few women had gathered around me, one even asking after if I understood the prayer. Life was thrust back into my bones as I stood in the altar.

That evening at midnight, I was very restless and drew a bath. As soon as I lowered myself into the tub, a cloud entered the room. I didn't know this could happen or what it was but I did know God was there, visiting me as a confirmation of the prayer that had been prayed in the afternoon. Unable to move, I spoke out loud, "Please don't leave me." The encounter may have lasted less than a minute but the memory will last forever.

It wasn't me who wanted to die that day. The depression wanted me to die, and so did the thief.

In the fall of 2010, I would have one more experience with this kind of spirit. Out of the blue one morning, the kids had left for school and I was going to take a few minutes and sit in our front room. All was well, and I was not low, but a voice that wasn't in my heart spoke to me. I knew I wasn't going crazy, and I knew it wasn't God. I was reminded of John 10:5, where it talks about how sheep know the voice of their shepherd and will never follow the voice of a stranger. Twice that morning I was given ideas of how to take my life, and a third time later that day occurred when I was out with my husband. I immediately shared with him what was happening and called a friend who was also a pastor, who then set up an appointment for deliverance ministry. I didn't know what that was or how it worked, but by the end of the session we had resolution. The focus had been on freemasonry, which I also had never heard of. The experience didn't scare me, and I believe God knew I was ready. I was stronger, it was the right time, and it is finished.

Marriage Vow Renewal

On October 21, 2008, my husband and I renewed our vows. Prior to this date, I had lost my engagement and wedding ring, which had been soldered together. It's not a great feeling to lose your rings. We had been talking about renewing our vows prior to this, and the missing rings contributed to our final decision to renew our vows and purchase new rings. We had been married fourteen years, spending the last five of those years as believers, and because of our decision to follow Jesus we wanted to officially invite Him into our marriage. A week or so had passed since losing my rings, and during a conversation, my husband shared the loss of my rings with his friend. His friend perked up, explaining he and his wife had been out walking and several times had stepped over sheets of paper on the ground, until he picked one of the papers up. The paper was a notice that someone had found a ring and left their phone number. I called the number and quickly discovered that my ring was in their possession.

I went to their home, and a man met me at the door with a large black dog. He explained that he had been on a walk with his dog when "suddenly" his dog ran off the bike path into the grass, sniffed around, and returned with my ring in his mouth. He thought maybe he had a present for his wife, but his wife insisted that someone would want this ring back. We were incredibly thankful to have the rings returned. This was not a path I lived near or walked on but I had been in the neighborhood around the time I had lost my rings. We even speculated maybe a bird had found the ring and dropped it near the path. However the ring had ended up in the grass, we were relieved and in awe of the return.

What's even more incredible is a few months prior to losing my ring, I'd had a dream. In the dream, I was bathing in a brilliant white tub in an all-white washroom. While I laid in the tub filled with bubbles, a large black dog walked in through the doorway straight towards me and thoroughly sniffed my face and neck.

The dream was surprising, considering I'm not completely comfortable with dogs.

You can imagine my astonishment when the man opened his door and introduced me to his large, black dog. The sniffing dog I had dreamed about months earlier found my rings. This dog had my scent. We loved the story even more when we asked our children what dog spelled backwards... "God."

We kept the original wedding ring, in which the imprint of the dog's teeth marks in the gold band can still be seen, and we purchased new rings for our vow renewal.

Our vow renewal was precious. In the ceremony, not without tears, we invited Jesus into our marriage. We had what we call our grown-up wedding. An intimate evening, with twenty-five friends surrounding us along with white candles lighting up the altar. Twinkling lights lit up the back of the room, hung over three round tables where we would enjoy a catered meal. White tablecloths, soft pink linens, and a small flower arrangement on each table were the touches to a special evening. A beautiful three-tier, elegantly decorated white banana-flavored cake, generously made for us by a friend, was enjoyed by all. We never intended for it to become what it did, but we were grateful. Our children participated in the ceremony, and we were blessed after dinner with kind words from every person in the room.

As the evening ended, we were pleased, and after everyone left, my husband and I sat together in the sanctuary, savoring the evening. Months later, we would find ourselves entering the toughest season of our marriage, but we had renewed our vows at the altar. Commitment kept us on track, God was faithful to shower us with much needed grace, and today we continue to enjoy the incredible blessings of marriage. My husband is my best friend, and I wouldn't want it any other way.

"And now these three remain: faith, hope and love.
But the greatest of these is love."[3]

ENDNOTES

1. Psalm 84:10 (NIV)
2. Ephesians 5:27 (NIV)
3. 1 Corinthians 13:13 (NIV)

CHAPTER SIX

HE HAS NOT GIVEN ME
A SPIRIT OF FEAR

"For God will never give you the spirit of cowardly fear, but he gives the Holy Spirit, who gives you mighty power, love, and a mind that has been delivered, protected, and secure".[1] At the beginning of 2017, I read this verse from *The Passion Translation* for the first time and a "yes" leaped in my spirit. I exchanged a "we did it!" with God. I love the words "delivered, protected, and secure."

This scripture was first spoken to me in 2004, the translation ending with the words "a sound mind." My response to hearing the scripture when I was unwell was that I must be less than and not good enough because my mind didn't seem sound. I didn't want to be seen in the church as a broken believer, so I distanced myself from the verse, and doing this allowed pride to hinder healing. My desire to be viewed as further along than I was wasn't entirely wrong, but resisting the Word and self-reliance was. God would teach me "when I am weak, then I am strong."[2]

Fear's goal is to disrupt life and cause everything it touches to blow out of proportion. It can leave a person scared, small, and restricted. For a time, fear seemed to have more power than the Holy Spirit I had invited into my life, but this façade ran its course, and as I continued to seek and enjoy God's presence, transformation happened.

Fear of a Familiar Feeling

Avoidance can be like a dance. A few shuffles forward, or a chassé can move you towards or away from a destination. Choosing to dance only on the left side of a room never allows you to experience the perspective from the right. Ultimately, dancing in such a way, or living life in such a way that permits avoidance robs us of freedom and an abundant life. When I received the miracle that relieved me of the panic attacks, I was content to now live in this new way. I couldn't imagine there was more. I couldn't imagine the wholeness and freedom God had for me to walk into, going from strength to strength, and He didn't want me to avoid any of it.

For example, I hadn't ridden a bike in several years. I had consciously stopped activities that required excessive movement because sometimes movement when I was unhealthy caused feelings of anxiety. Even though my well-being had increased, my physical body and soul still held memories of darker days. I was never fearful of bike riding, but I had made the decision to avoid those things that would trigger the unwanted feelings. I could have lived out my life never riding a bike again, but that's not freedom.

I wanted to stop the avoidance dance and made the decision to ride my bike. It sounded simple, until a sudden, wave of anxiety rushed through my body as I pedaled my bike along a ravine. This seemed absurd until my feelings began to distract me from experiencing and enjoying the freedom of biking outdoors. I could have jumped off the bike to avoid the feeling, or push through the feeling and keep going. I kept going, and this is no longer an issue I live with. Fear doesn't discriminate by the size or caliber of a situation. If it can show up, it will.

Another movement related example is jazzercise classes, which I used to participate in. Eventually, I stopped going because of the unhealthy barrage of feelings I would experience during the class. Jumping up and down, moving side to side, the loud music, and the people caused anxiety. Again, I wasn't afraid of an exercise class but wanted to avoid the feelings. Today, I can jump and dance in the altar of our church, with God and I knowing how far I have come.

During the time I was unwell, my husband and I went to see an action movie. The extreme noise from the movie overloaded my senses. I lay in bed most of that night fearing the sounds that echoed in my mind. The visit that night to the movies may have happened too early in my healing journey, but allowing years to go by before considering the return to the theatres was part of the avoidance dance. No one wants to repeat a negative experience, and I certainly didn't. Returning to the theatre did trigger low levels of anxiety, but again, I wasn't fearful of the movie theatre but the feelings. The reward of the return is now being able to enjoy an occasional date night at the movies with my husband.

Avoiding any type of shopping venues such as malls, outlets, and grocery stores was very limiting. Intentional, unwanted trips were necessary before building up to the ease they hold today. Malls that once triggered an upset stomach, hampered decision making, and caused extreme lightheadedness, I can walk into without thinking twice. Grocery store shopping that used to leave me scattered is now enjoyable, especially when I am thankful for the choices and the provision to shop, and if I forget an item, it's ok.

Recently, I was walking through a mall, and where fear had once ruled, I was overcome by how straightforward and normal this trip had become. Tears filled my eyes as I embraced peace and was reminded once again it's always more than we can think or imagine.

Fear of Flying

In 2008, our family was planning a trip to attend a church conference in Hawaii. This was a big deal. I would fly for the first time after walking off a plane with my baby girl in my arms in 1996. We had successfully flown to our destination but as I sat waiting in my seat for the return trip home, the urgency to get off had the final say. My very patient and loving husband decided to turn that moment into an adventure even though we had no vehicle or clothes and limited funds to get home. However, agreeing with fear instead of freedom had me choosing not to board a plane for twelve years, until Hawaii.

As a family of five, this trip was an investment financially and a time to create memories. For days leading up to the flight, my body responded to stress with bizarre physical symptoms. When the anticipated arrival of boarding our first flight had finally arrived, I took my seat, buckled up, and immediately began to picture walking off the plane as I had years earlier. The tug of war was real, but my soundness kept me seated, along with prayer and the desire not to give in to fear in front of my three children.

A man leaned across the aisle and handed me a pamphlet. The pamphlet was from a Christian mission organization with a cover showing a boy jumping on an island under a palm tree. The words surrounding the boy were "joy," "love," and "peace." I held that pamphlet tight, a kiss from God, as we flew the one-hour flight to our destination without a hitch.

We passed through customs and I began to feel unwell quickly and soon enough had a fever. By the time we took our seats in the boarding area I was very unwell. I apologetically let my husband know I couldn't go any further. Disappointment set in and my husband spoke with the airline about our options. We were informed a flight would be leaving in a couple of days with room for our family, if we chose to continue. We were escorted back through customs, uncertain whether our journey had come to an end.

Tucked in a hotel bed, the decision not to continue seemed to be easy to make. We entertained canceling the six-hour flight, and once again the avoidance dance was dancing me back home. A call to our church for support revealed the next flight available would be the same one our pastors and their family would be on. This helped us make the decision to continue. It was God's way of leading me through a fight I needed to win.

The fever eventually broke, and feeling about sixty percent better, we returned to the airport. Our pastors greeted us upon our arrival, and we prayed. In the healing season I was in, having our pastors and their family on board the plane was a comfort.

As we sat waiting in the boarding area, my name was announced over the loud speaker to receive a call at the airline's desk. Who would be calling me at the airport? I went to the desk, picked up the phone, and heard the voice of a young woman who had helped us at the desk two days before. She was calling from another desk across the airport. She let me know she had been praying for us and wanted to be sure we had returned, and to wish us a great trip. She also wanted to let me know that a flight attendant returning home to Hawaii would be seated next to me if I had any questions about the plane. God was continuing to take care of me.

We boarded the plane, and it was announced the pilot's mom was on board, so it would be a smooth flight. My pastor, with continued care, walked down the aisle to check on me before take-off. It really is daily, simple exchanges we do for one another that make a difference. After take-off, I spent the next six hours chatting with the off-duty flight attendant, about her beliefs and God, only asking her two questions about the plane, which she answered thoroughly.

We arrived at the Hawaii airport, and it was a smooth flight. Walking toward baggage, our pastors walked towards us, and she gave me a big mom-like type hug. When we acknowledge and celebrate each other's victories, we all win. What is easy for one may be difficult for another, but love can bridge the gap.

God stayed close, encouraging me by His Spirit and other people. If you're wondering what the return trip was like, it was uneventful, almost as if I had been flying my whole life.

Fear of Man

"Am I now trying to win the approval of human beings, or of God? Or am I trying to please people? If I were still trying to please people, I would not be a servant of Christ"[3]

The fear of man is ridiculous, but it has been one of my most personally frustrating fears I have had to face, particularly in the church. This fear can have you going around the mountain numerous times if you don't settle the why. Why are you scared of people?

God desires to enlarge our tents, expand us,[4] and I believe this happens when our willingness works together with His will. When we respond in fear towards one another, we can potentially withhold and restrict the power of the Holy Spirit, who wants to be expressed through us. I have deliberately had to push beyond feelings of insecurity and rejection to stop the fear of man from shutting me down. When I do this, the Spirit of God is free to move in greater ways in my life. Sometimes we determine our breakthrough by our actions, and we can do this because God already has said numerous times not to fear.

For example, I regularly attend weekly church prayer meetings. It's a gathering I look forward to attending, and participating in. For a time, this changed. This fear of man I struggled with was being challenged and escalated to the point that prayer meeting after meeting would pass without my contribution. The inability to walk up to the front and pray had a strong grip on me. After a few months, I noticed this fear began to find its way into conversations with people. My ability to express myself well began to diminish, and frustration set in.

Despite this turning into a weekly battle, I was determined to keep showing up. It was as if I was sitting in a vehicle at a four-way stop and kept missing my turn because the person to my right, left, or straight ahead took their turns without me. Then the thought came, the person behind me can't go, unless I go. We spur one another on, we can pave the way for each other, and I believe God is happy when we do. Over the years, the Holy Spirit, has given me many green lights to contribute and take my turn. Sometimes I have held back from an opportunity, whispering "I'm sorry" to Him afterwards. Other times I have asked God, "Can we try again?" Remember, what is easy for one, can be difficult for another, but love can bridge the gap.

We're not unified, if we fear one another. "How good and pleasant it is when God's people live together in unity!"[5] There is much we can do together:

Let's be molded and shaped into His image, not a man-made image.
Let's be super-courageous when using our gifts.
Let's be excellent encouragers and build His church.
Let's be generous and watch it multiply.
Let's be wise and extend our reach into the world.

Stability

During the summer of 2012, I attended a one-week school at Bethel Church, in Redding, CA. I cherish this trip and my time spent there. I value the teaching and encountering His presence but what changed me was a personal gift received from God while there. On day two of the school, an unusual awareness came upon me. I noticed I felt different, stable and steady. A strength was touching my mind, and as the week progressed, it occurred to me that living life with this stability could be possible.

After an incredible week, we began the lengthy drive home, and throughout the trip, I continued to be aware of the feeling. However, when we crossed into our city limits, I felt the stability lift. I was confused and wondered what had just happened. I don't always understand the why, but I knew this time I had tasted something that was meant to be mine, and I wanted it to return permanently.

We had also entered a season that challenged my emotional stability at a new level. I would learn how to manage my emotions over the next three years, which would mature my character, my walk with the Lord and with people. I can see now how this was a next step to wholeness. I was no longer debilitated by fear and no longer struggling with depression but needed to learn how to submit my emotions to God. For everything I thought had gone wrong in this season, much had gone right. It's important and healthy to recognize the wins and continue to give thanks for how far you've come.

When this season did come to an end, I needed to hear from God. I sat before Him, prayed, and waited. As I was about to stand up, He spoke, "I'm anchoring you." The Bible says, "We have this hope as an anchor for the soul, firm and secure. It enters the inner sanctuary behind the curtain."[6]

The stability I experienced at Bethel returned and I am living more anchored than I have ever been. Peace-filled days will outnumber all the days spent in fear.

ENDNOTES

1. 2 Timothy 1:7 (TPT)
2. 2 Corinthians 12:10 (NIV)
3. Galatians 1:10 (NIV)
4. Isaiah 54:2 (NIV)
5. Psalm 133:1 (NIV)
6. Hebrews 6:19 (NIV)

CHAPTER SEVEN
LETTING GO TO LIVE FREE

Crossing the Jordan was not possible without supernatural intervention from God.[1]

The Bible says the water had stopped flowing and piled up in a heap a great distance away, allowing Israel to cross over. Can you even imagine what that looked like? An entire nation was let go to walk a way they had never been.

My healing hasn't happened solely because I worked hard to get better, though I have. I needed God to intervene. The waters needed to part to enter my promise land. I knew it, and God knew it. But to get there, He did require that I let go. I believe that once you cross over, you can look back and remember a familiar place, but God will not part the waters for your return. "So, if the son sets you free, you will be free indeed."[2]

Letting Go of Clutter

I find pleasure in bringing order to a chaotic closet, disorganized cupboard, or an overflowing drawer. Deciding what to keep, pass on, or throw away is an opportunity for change.

Over time, that same closet may require some refreshing such as refolding a sheet or throwing out a well-used blanket. The less that is allowed to accumulate in the closet, partnered with maintaining a reasonable amount of order, prevents unnecessary time spent on the closet.

At times, my mind may have looked like a cluttered closet overflowing with fears, worries, disappointments, and everything else that could possibly be stuffed inside.

> The fruit of letting go of my clutter has been a renewed and quiet mind.

Letting Go of Me

Letting go of me began with forgiving myself for the past and decisions that were not God's best for my life. Forgiving myself has also removed the ropes of regret I had been tied to for too long. The regret that had impacted me the most was having been an unhealthy mom for a time, a season that seemed to last too long and had me wondering too often if I could have been a better mom.

Not long ago during an evening of reflection, my husband let me know I had been a great mom and how capable I had been despite the measuring stick I used and what I had walked through. He was right. There had been a lot I had done very well, and it's freeing to be able to admit success during an adverse time.

> The fruit of letting go of me has been getting to know me.

Letting Go of Others

Fixing my eyes on Jesus has empowered me to let go of offense, disappointment, pain, and misunderstanding accumulated from relationships over the years. No matter how small or significant a situation seemed, it all needed to go, everything, and occasionally more than once.

When my husband and I lock eyes, an established bond of love and trust exists between us, which moves us forward, as one, in marriage. Time spent fixing my eyes on Jesus establishes that same bond of love and trust, securing us so I can see what He sees. From this I am growing a greater ability to see situations, circumstances, and people with a more accurate and healthy perspective.

Jesus set a precedent for a way of living when he hung on the cross and said, "Father, forgive them, for they do not know what they are doing." And they divided up His clothes by casting lots.[3] What seems inconsiderate and uncompassionate apparently wasn't to those in the moment. I don't want a "what can I get out of this situation" attitude, but rather I would like the heart and perspective Jesus had as He released words that have marked and blessed mankind for all time.

When we stop fighting ourselves, others, and God, we can receive that same perspective. I have watched with my spiritual eyes, words intended to harm me slide across my heart and not enter. It's possible to not receive a wound, but if it does, I fix my eyes on Him and forgive as I have been forgiven.

> The fruit of letting go of others is love.

Letting Go For God

"Now the Lord is the Spirit, and where the Spirit of the Lord is, there is freedom."[4]

As a consistent dreamer, I look forward to recording my dreams. On the eve of October 26, 2011, just before falling asleep, I was expectant and hopeful to dream, eager to find out if God had a message for the following day, my birthday. He did, and the message has continued to be timeless and relatable.

In the dream, I was at some type of party or celebration. A woman I knew, represented the Holy Spirit. I watched her descend a flight of stairs wearing a silvery cocktail dress, cut just above her knees, and sparkly high heeled shoes on her feet. Walking with a bounce and a huge smile on her face, she made her way over to me, engaging with others along the way. Once close enough, we hugged and rocking back and forth she whispered in my ear, "Loosen up."

"Loosen up" wasn't entirely a part of my vocabulary. I knew I needed to but didn't know how—or more accurately, hadn't allowed myself to loosen up in a long time. I'm unable to gauge how much loosening up happened that year, but the Lord was calling me to transition into greater freedom. He was calling me to laugh more, dance more, relax more, love more, and overall enjoy life more. As parents, we delight when our children laugh together, act goofy, joke, and carry on, and God has given us permission to relax or as my kids might say "chill".

> The fruit of letting go for God is pleasure.

Letting Go in Prayer

In January of 2006, I attended my first corporate prayer meeting at church. The first few Tuesday evenings, I observed from a chair at the back of the room. Many of us seem to choose the back of a room when new.

Up to this point, my experience with prayer had been primarily solitary. While we attended the Lutheran Church, for months I would spend thirty minutes most mornings in the prayer room of the church after dropping my girls off at school. My son would play under the bench I sat on with a car, while I listened for God's voice. This is what I knew prayer to be. Some mornings were spent not hearing one word, and other mornings, one word heard was enough.

Praying with others would be a welcome change. That first evening, as I observed from the back of the sanctuary, soaking music playing from the speakers, some sat, some stood, and others laid face down in the altar. For the next few years, I looked forward to these nights, eventually finding myself face down at the altar with a journal by my side. Admittedly, I was sometimes more aware of what others thought than Him.

Experiencing God and soaking in His presence week after week in those early years was precious. I can't even fathom all He did in me during that time.

> The fruit of letting go in prayer is intimacy.

Letting Go in Worship

During my early Sunday worship experiences at the Lutheran Church, I remember sneaking glances at a woman who often stood mid-center of the sanctuary. Watching her raise her hands and rhythmically move them to the music intrigued me. In fact, I took note early on that she and the worship leader were sometimes, not all the time, the only ones with raised hands during the worship time.

As a new believer, I noticed that the psalms spoke of dancing, clapping, and shouting and had me wondering why I was only seeing this from a few. Their freedom, whether perceived as weird or not the norm, beckoned me to give it a try. However, self-consciousness allowed church culture to influence me back then more than the Bible itself.

In our next church community, individuals did raise their hands, and so a new journey began. Letting go in worship would bring me closer to His heart, His presence, and His freedom. At first, letting go looked like placing my right-hand palm up where no one could see. Bravery meant lifting my hand, palm up, waist high. Eventually, one arm raised head height, would lead to both arms raised head height. I hope you see where this is leading. Again, I was self-conscious and way too concerned about what people would think.

I think we can be fooled into believing the process is more difficult than it needs to be, causing us to stall along the way. We stall because there is an enemy-driven assignment in the spirit to slow us down. But where the Spirit of the Lord is, freedom is accessible, whether we reach out for it a little at a time or all at once.

Worship music combined with God's presence is a powerful healing combination. When my mind was too anxious to read the Bible, pray, or actively engage in worship, I could still listen to worship music. Sitting under, being immersed in, and saturating our home with hours and hours of worship music released by gifted men and women is an easy and life-changing gift to receive.

The Bible talks about Paul and Silas praying and singing to God at midnight after they had been severely flogged, locked in an inner cell with their feet fastened in the stocks. Despite pain and being confined, they chose to worship God together, and as they did the other prisoners listened. As they communed with the One they loved, sudden, supernatural intervention caused the prison doors to fly open and everyone's chains to loosen.

Letting go in worship during adversity influenced heaven and earth. An entire household was saved. "The jailer brought them into his house and set a meal before them; he was filled with joy because he had come to believe in God—he and his whole household." [5]

The fruit of letting go in worship is freedom.

More Joy

For years, genuine joy eluded me. Smiling and an occasional laugh weren't non-existent, but over time the laughter became fleeting. I have always admired those who laugh outrageously. The infectious kind of laugh that commands your attention and has the potential to even offend the serious.

When my husband and I were first married, we were youthful goofballs, laughing over ridiculous situations that only he and I would find funny. An onlooker could very well have perceived us as immature in those days, which may have been an accurate observation, but we were happy.

Over time, life seemed to get serious, with responsibilities, maturing, the addition of children, finances, and maintaining a home all contributed to the increase of my anxiety. But Jesus hung on the cross to change that scenario for you and me, promising that joy comes in the morning.

I am well acquainted with crying. I have been known to cry when sad, happy, frustrated, moved by His Spirit, listening to a true story, when someone else cries, and for no apparent reason. This is probably not an exhaustive list. More recently, I have also become sensitive to occasional weeping during times of personal change. I'm learning to recognize and withdraw as needed when this happens, not to hide, but to give the process some space.

I used to pray that I wouldn't cry so easily in front of people, and the answer to that prayer seemed to be crying more often. My response to this is to become an unapologetic crier. Tears can be refreshing, and when partnered with letting go, can make room for joy, allowing the soul to find expression and freely flow. The opposite of crying is laughter, and the first few times I laughed enthusiastically for no apparent reason, with my face contorted and tears streaming down my face, was bizarre but so good.

"You turned my wailing into dancing; you removed my sackcloth and clothed me with joy, that my heart may sing your praises and not be silent. Lord my God I will praise you forever."[6]

The fruit of joy is victory.

ENDNOTES

1. Joshua 3 (NIV)
2. John 8:36 (NIV)
3. Luke 23:34 (NIV)
4. 2 Corinthians 3:17 (NIV)
5. Acts 16:25-34 (NIV)
6. Psalm 30:11 (NIV)

CHAPTER EIGHT
TIME TO FLY

In June 2015, eleven years had passed since hearing God's direction to "go to the church" and pray in the small library on a dark, confusing day. This local, longstanding church was strategically placed by God in the heart of what could be called a thriving community—a local church not unlike many others in our communities, towns, and cities that could seemingly go unnoticed to the public passing by on their way to work, home, school, or the store. I used to be one of those passers-by.

But on a not-so-ordinary day, as others passed by, that building became more than a building and took on more meaning than I may ever be able to express, because God was there. As I sat in the library surrounded by stories and pages filled with words, I had no idea He was authoring mine, and eleven years later He was adding another chapter to my story.

Once Upon a Vision

I was spending the day with a friend browsing an outdoor market, located in a small town near the city. We enjoyed lunch together and shopped. We shopped for friends and ourselves. My favorite purchase was large blocks spelling out the word FAMILY for our front foyer.

During our return trip to the city, we decided to enjoy the scenic route as worship music played in the back ground. Approaching another small town, my friend asked if I was in a hurry to get home. I was not. She parked in front of a stretch of stores and pointed out a photography studio she had visited before. A random stop was about to become not so random.

I can imagine angels positioned on either side of the door, waiting for us to enter in anticipation of what God would reveal. Stepping into the store, my eyes scanned the various photos of animals hanging on the walls, and suddenly it occurred to me, there could be an eagle in the room. Asking the owner, he directed me to an eagle section. My hand flipped through the photographs, and my heart skipped a beat as my eyes fell on a picture, the vision of the eagle from once upon a time. Eleven years had passed. Eleven years of hoping that maybe one day I would hold a picture of the vision I had seen in my hands.

This part of my journey was coming full circle. It was time to transition, and I knew it. The moment was significant and surreal as the eagle stared back at me in all its strength, reminding me how alive God's promise was inside of me. I hadn't set out that morning thinking about my past or my future. I was simply spending an unsuspecting day with a friend when "suddenly" He stepped in.

© Branded Visuals – Robert G. Cook
(used with permission)
www.brandedvisuals.com

I purchased a matted print of the eagle, and we headed home. I was thankful to share this moment with my friend and very excited to show this present from God with my family. At the end of a wonderful day, I placed the print on a chair in the room where we intended to hang the picture and headed to bed. For the next few days, the print stayed in the bag on the chair. My husband inquired why we weren't hanging the picture. I wasn't sure but did know that something felt unfinished.

That week, our church hosted a conference called, Dominion Conference which I felt was significant on behalf of Canada. I sat in the first session, and God spoke to my heart to give the eagle picture to the conference founders. I had waited a long time to have this picture but was not surprised to be giving it away. I went home between sessions, returned to the conference with the picture, and did what I felt God had asked and gave it away. I was thankful for the opportunity but still sensed something was unfinished.

During worship, a guest speaker stood and declared from the platform, "An eagle army is rising in Canada." Her words had my full attention. I'm uncertain at what point the eagle picture had been placed between two Canada flags on the platform but I was astonished when I noticed.

No one in the room would have suspected what happened to my heart that day. All the times I had looked to heaven and whispered, "I know that you know," I was whispering it again. Not because I was in the dark but because I was completely in the light. My first vision, from one of my darkest days, was now being displayed in the altar representing a conference for Canada. A country who carries a prophetic destiny, "And the leaves of the tree are for the healing of the nations."[1]

Waiting until the room emptied, I stood at the back of the room to sneak one last private glance at the picture. Wiping tears from my eyes, I remained long enough for my open heart and sound mind to give thanks. This seemed to be the end to a part of my story just as I had read many times about others —good overcoming evil, and the final chapter signing off with "The End."

Agreement with The Future

Gone are the days spent meditating on a future I couldn't see. Instead, I am well able to sit before God, dream about what life could bring, think on the promises His Word has left for us all, and with expectancy ask about my todays and tomorrows, believing, that endless opportunities do exist.

In 2016, I attended another conference in our city. We are fortunate as a city to host many great conferences. At the end of the first evening, the guest speaker walked up to me and shook my hand, an attention-catching handshake. At the end of the second evening, we were face to face once again, and this time as he reached out and shook my hand he spoke, "Sometimes we shake hands, when we greet one another or when we're meeting for the first time. Other times we shake hands in agreement with what God is doing. I'm shaking your hand in agreement with what God is doing in your life and God himself is shaking your hand in agreement with your life."

God agreed with my future and so should I. My part was to give Him my yes, to all the God-given desires in my heart, changing "doubt" to "do" in a moment. I know God removes any need to wander miserably and aimlessly in this life. Every time I am invited by a family to pray and prophesy over new life, my expectancy level rises for each new generation, believing every baby from the onset should have multiple yes's spoken into and over their life, saturating the atmosphere around each one with heaven.

I spent a long time not liking myself, and I know being able to agree with my future and co-labor with Christ says lovingly back to my Father, "Thank you for creating me."

Beautiful Timing

"He has made everything beautiful in its time. He has also set eternity in the human heart; yet no one can fathom what God has done from beginning to end."[2]

Where we live, many months of winter aren't unusual, so the first signs of spring breaking through the ground are eagerly anticipated by many. The waiting welcomes a needed season change, but if a flower were to peek through the ground in the middle of a blizzard, chances would be it wouldn't survive. But when the temperature is right and the soil has softened, that carefully hidden flower gets to break forth into the light and grow just at the right time. Trusting God allows our hearts to trust His timing. He knows what's best for us and when.

During the second week of writing, as I sat in our front room praying and dreaming about how to put this book together, a leak from an upstairs toilet that I could not hear was causing significant water damage to our home. Restoration and renovation is messy, and there are no shortcuts. Wet ceilings, floors and beams needed to be exposed, and a thorough drying-out process was necessary. If a wet wall were to remain hidden, it could eventually produce mold and rot the wood. The process sounds similar to what can happen in our own lives.

Each step of the restoration has meant coordinating the right people at the right time to help make things new, all working in their areas of expertise. You don't want a painter laying a floor down if they don't know how, and you don't want flooring replaced before the ceiling. Some weeks we wouldn't see a lot of progress and suddenly we would see a lot. You wouldn't want a job half-done on your home, so neither should we settle for a job half-done on our lives. The fruit of the Spirit called patience was required, and after four months of renovations our home is beautiful.

I had regretted time spent unwell but the Lord had something else in mind for all the time that had gone by:

"To bestow on them a crown of beauty instead of ashes,
the oil of joy instead of mourning, and a garment of praise
instead of a spirit of despair.
They will be called oaks of righteousness, a planting of the
Lord for the display of his splendor." [3]

Our crowns are beautiful.

Finding and Building My Voice

"What I tell you in the dark, speak in the daylight; what is
whispered in your ear, proclaim from the roofs."[4]

How wonderful that what He whispers, we can proclaim but it is difficult to proclaim if you haven't found your voice. Finding my voice has meant discovering and embracing my unique sound. Building my voice has meant learning how to articulate my thoughts, feelings, and ideas with clarity, strength, and grace.

I believe it's not always about the amount of words we speak, but how and what we speak, and even then, sometimes the most powerful thing we can say is nothing. Our words, our messages, and our conversations benefit by being submitted to God so we can speak to one another as it is written, "Let your conversations be always full of grace, seasoned with salt, so that you may know how to answer everyone."[5]

Living with an Open Heart

Many weekends have passed since the Holy Spirit weekend away when I said yes to Jesus and He supernaturally opened my heart to Him and the world around me. I may have remained in an unlocked prison for a little while, hiding my heart, but just as my husband had coaxed me to cross the threshold of our home when I was unwell, God coaxed me back to life.

The young woman who thought she was crazy, slouched low in the passenger seat of her car, had determined this was no way to live, and she was right. This wasn't the way to live, but she couldn't see a decade down the road. She couldn't see she wouldn't always remain a fearful passenger, her hand gripping the door, hanging on for dear life. God had a love plan for this young woman, and at the perfect time, He moved her over to the driver's seat, directing her to continue to follow freedom. She bravely took the wheel, and with a quick glance in the rearview mirror, she could see she was leaving fear far behind.

> "You satisfy my every desire with good things.
> You've supercharged my life so that I soar again
> Like a flying eagle in the sky."[6]

The End

ENDNOTES

1. Revelations 22:2 (NIV)
2. Ecclesiastes 3:11 (NIV)
3. Isaiah 61:3 (NIV)
4. Matthew 10:27 (NIV)
5. Colossians 4:6 (NIV)
6. Psalm 103:5 (TPT)

WORKS CITED

Brian Doerksen. "The River." 2008.

The Holy Bible, New International Version. Grand Rapids, MI: Zondervan, 2011.

Special Edition 2-in-1 Collection of The Psalms: Poetry on Fire and Proverbs: Wisdom, The Passion Translation with 31-Day Psalms and Proverbs Devotionals. Racine, WI: BroadStreet Publishing Group, LLC, 2015.

"Trust." Merriam-Webster.com. Merriam-Webster, n.d. Web. 28 June 2017.

"Perseverance." Merriam-Webster.com. Merriam-Webster, n.d. Web. 28 June 2017.

U2. *"Stuck In a Moment You Can't Get Out Of."* Hanover Quay Studios, Dublin, 2000.

ABOUT THE AUTHOR

Deborah McCafferty lives and breathes her testimony of God's healing power over anxiety, panic, fear and depression. It is because of this miracle journey that she willingly and transparently shares her story with others who are in the throes of this often private battle.

Now, as an emerging author and communicator, Deborah's heart is to offer hope and inspiration to those suffering that it IS possible to be set free and that life can be more than we ask or imagine. She has a passion for spending time in God's presence and encourages others in this practice as well because of the powerful transformation it faithfully provides.

Deborah is a wife, and mother of three. She loves the beach, walking, and family time around the dinner table. She and her family reside in Calgary, Alberta.

To Connect with Deborah, visit:
www.DeborahMcCafferty.com